Unusual Pets

HISSING COCKROACHES

MARYSA STORM

BLACK RABBIT BOOKS

Bolt is published by Black Rabbit Books
P.O. Box 227, Mankato, Minnesota, 56002.
www.blackrabbitbooks.com

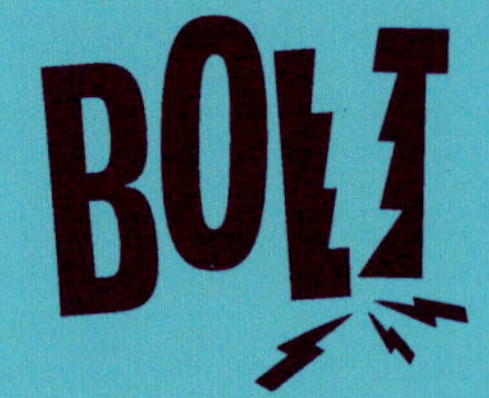

Alissa Thielges, editor; Rhea Magaro, designer and photo researcher

Library of Congress Cataloging-in-Publication Data
Names: Storm, Marysa, author.
Title: Hissing cockroaches / by Marysa Storm.
Description: Mankato, MN: Bolt is published by Black Rabbit Books, [2026] | Series: Unusual pets | Includes bibliographical references and index. | Audience: Ages 8-12 | Audience: Grades 4-6
Identifiers: LCCN 2024043366 (print) | LCCN 2024043367 (ebook) | ISBN 9781644667798 (library binding) | ISBN 9781644667910 (ebook)
Subjects: LCSH: Madagascar hissing cockroach—Juvenile literature.
Classification: LCC QL505.7.B4 S76 2026 (print) | LCC QL505.7.B4 (ebook) | DDC 595.7/28—dc23/eng/20241213
LC record available at https://lccn.loc.gov/2024043366

Image Credits

Alamy Stock Photo/ blickwinkel/B. Trapp, 9; Dreamstime/ Alessandrozocc, 25, Ruslan Grigolava, 18–19, Troichenko, 4-5; Shutterstock/Aastels, 16–17, 24, Al More, cover, Alexey Stiop, 1, Anna Tsygankova, 26–27, Ceren Bayrak, 4-5, Connie Wade, 19, dropStock, 24–25, Eric Isselee, 28–29, Guillermo Guerao Serra, 13, Iv-olga, 21, JIANG HONGYAN, 25, JJJW, 24, Ljupco Smokovski, 13, LouieLea, 8, PRO Stock Professional, 26–27, Protasov AN, 31, Pum Story, 25, Robert Eastman, 11, skydie, 3, 15, TH2I Shutter Rich, cover, torook, 22, Vera Larina, 6–7, 2happy, 32; Wikimedia Commons/Matt Reinbold, 21

CONTENTS

CHAPTER 1

Meet the HISSING COCKROACH

A young girl is curled up on her sofa, reading. Suddenly, she notices something moving. It's a giant, shiny bug. And it's climbing up the curtains! The girl is not scared though. Instead, she laughs. She knows this critter. It's her pet!

In the wild, hissing cockroaches live in groups called colonies.

Crawly Friend

The girl holds her palms up in front of the bug. It crawls onto her hands. The girl walks slowly. She heads toward the bug's **terrarium**. As she goes, the roach travels from one hand to another. Its legs tickle her palms. Its antennae move to find new smells.

CHAPTER 2

A SPECIAL PET

A hissing cockroach isn't an ordinary pet. It isn't even an ordinary insect! These unique bugs come from the island Madagascar. There, they crawl around the forest floor. They come out at night. They eat fallen fruits and veggies.

Madagascar is hot and **humid**.

WHERE HISSING COCKROACHES LIVE IN THE WILD

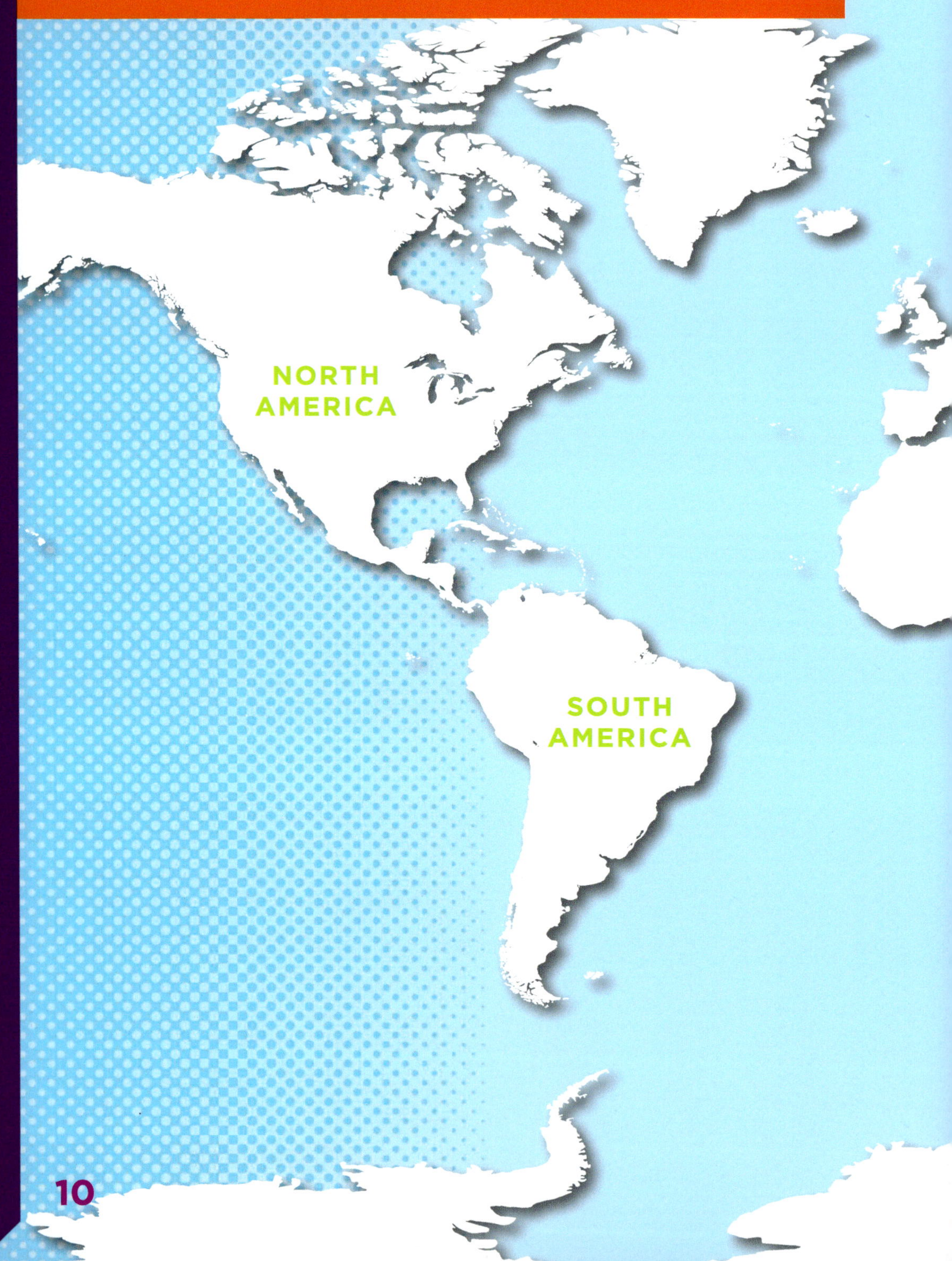

EUROPE
ASIA
AFRICA
AUSTRALIA
MADAGASCAR
ANTARCTICA

CHAPTER 3

Hissing Cockroach

These insects are large. They usually grow to 2 to 3 inches (5 to 7.6 centimeters) long. Males are bigger than females. They have thicker antennae and larger horns too.

These bugs don't have wings. That means they can't fly. But they can climb! Spikes on their legs help them crawl up almost any surface.

Average Size

LENGTH
2 to 3
INCHES
(5 to 7.6 cm)
0 1 2 3 4 5 6 7 8 9 10
ounces
ounces
WEIGHT
less than
0.8
OUNCE
(22.6 grams)

Hiss! Hiss!

These bugs get their names from the sound they make. They often hiss when they are in danger. Males also hiss as a **mating** call. The sound is made through their breathing holes. The bugs force air out these openings.

COMPARING LENGTHS

Brown-banded cockroach

American cockroach

Hissing cockroach

Giant burrowing cockroach

length in inches

about 0.5 (1.3 cm)
about 1.5 (3.8 cm)
about 3 (7.6 cm)
about 3.2 (8.1 cm)

PARTS OF A HISSING COCKROACH

OVAL-SHAPED BODY
ANTENNAE
LARGE HORNS (MALES ONLY)

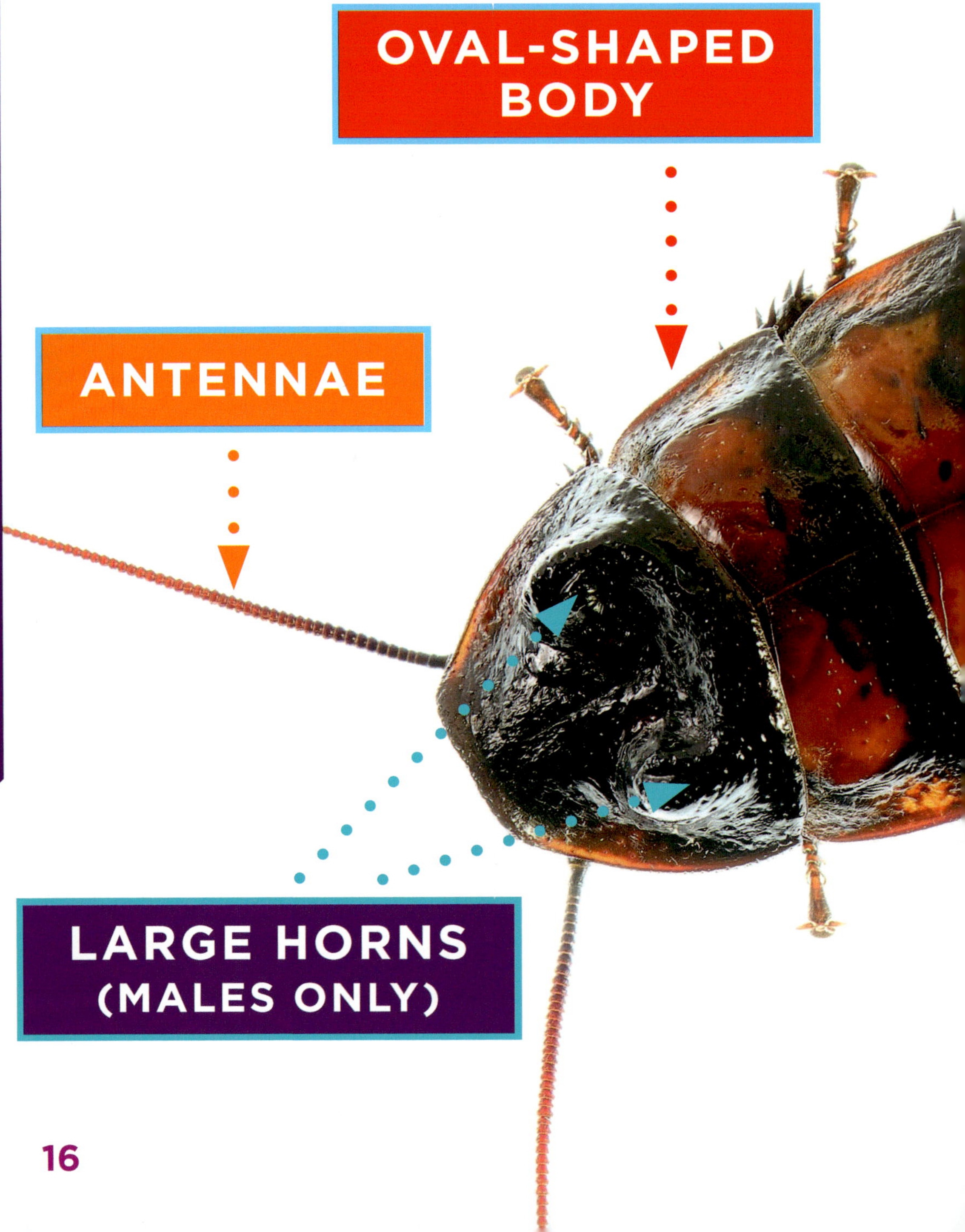

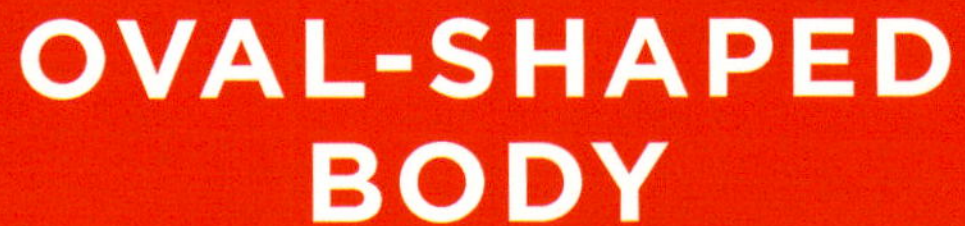

BREATHING HOLES
SPINY LEGS

CHAPTER 4

Caring for a HISSING COCKROACH

Hissing cockroaches are good starter pets. They are easy to take care of. Like most pets, they need food and fresh water daily. A small, shallow dish of water is best. Most owners feed their roaches a fruit and vegetable mix. Any uneaten food should be removed after 24 hours.

Good Foods

STORE-BOUGHT FOOD MIX

LEAFY GREENS

romaine lettuce, kale, collared greens

OVERRIPE FRUIT

apples, bananas, oranges

VEGETABLES

squash, carrots

Escape Artists

A terrarium makes a good home for these roaches. It is important to make sure the **mesh** lids fits well. Roaches are great climbers. They might get out if the lid is not on tight.

A hissing cockroach can be kept alone. Or you can keep them in a small group. However, owners with many roaches may end up with baby roaches.

Baby hissing roaches are called **nymphs.**

Like the Forest Floor

The tank should **mimic** a forest floor. The bottom should have a layer of bedding. There should be plenty of places to hide too. Logs, plants, and rocks are good additions. The plants should not be **toxic**. Owners can also add tubes for climbing.

A HISSING COCKROACH TANK

shallow water dish

logs, branches, or other plants

bedding
rocks
tubes

A Happy Home

Hissing cockroaches like hot and humid places. Their tank should be misted often. This keeps **moisture** in the air. A tank heater can help keep the tank hot.

It can take extra work to keep these critters happy. But owners love these unique pets. They are unlike any other!

THE RIGHT TEMPERATURE

Active
above 85°F (29°C)

Best day temperatures
80–85°F (27–29°C)

Best night temperatures
70–80°F (21–27°C)

Slow and sluggish
65–70°F (18–21°C)

Not safe
below 65°F (18°C)

100
80
60
40
20
0

By the

12 feet
(3.7 meters)
how far away a roach's hiss can be heard

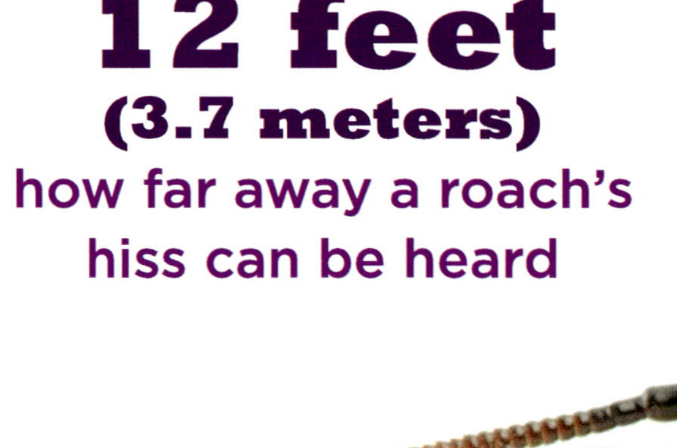

5 gallons
(19 liters)

GOOD SIZE FOR A COCKROACH TERRARIUM

about

4,000

NUMBER OF COCKROACH SPECIES THERE ARE

up to

60

HOW MANY NYMPHS ONE FEMALE COCKROACH CAN HAVE AT ONE TIME

up to

5

YEARS

HOW LONG A HISSING COCKROACH CAN LIVE

GLOSSARY

humid (hyoo-MID)—having a lot of moisture in the air

mate (MAYT)—to join together to produce young

mesh (MESH)—a material made from threads or wires with evenly spaced holes that allow air or water to pass through

mimic (MIM-ik)—to copy or resemble closely

moisture (MOYS-chur)—a small amount of liquid that makes something wet

nymph (NIMPF)—a young insect that has almost the same form as the adult

terrarium (tuh-RAIR-ee-uhm)—a glass or plastic box that is used for growing plants or keeping small animals indoors

toxic (TOK-sik)—poisonous

BOOKS

Gitlin, Marty. *Hissing Cockroaches.* Mankato, MN: Black Rabbit Books, 2020.

Humphrey, Natalie. *Hissing Cockroaches*. Buffalo, NY: Gareth Stevens Publishing, 2025.

WEBSITES

Hissing Cockroach
kids.nationalgeographic.com/animals/invertebrates/facts/hissing-cockroach

Madagascar Hissing Cockroach
www.marylandzoo.org/animal/madagascar-hissing-cockroach/

Madagascar Hissing Cockroach
www.sfzoo.org/madagascar-hissing-cockroach/

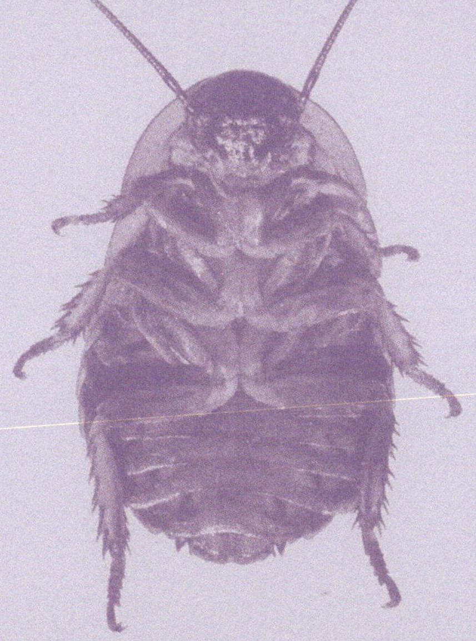

INDEX

ANIMAL BATTLES

MANDRILL VS. CHIMPANZEE

BY NATHAN SOMMER

TORQUE™

BELLWETHER MEDIA • MINNEAPOLIS, MN

Torque brims with excitement perfect for thrill-seekers of all kinds. Discover daring survival skills, explore uncharted worlds, and marvel at mighty engines and extreme sports. In *Torque* books, anything can happen. Are you ready?

This edition first published in 2025 by Bellwether Media, Inc.

Library of Congress Cataloging-in-Publication Data

LC record for Mandrill vs. Chimpanzee available at: https://lccn.loc.gov/2024036213

Editor: Suzane Nguyen Designer: Hunter Demmin

Printed in the United States of America, North Mankato, MN.

TABLE OF CONTENTS

THE COMPETITORS

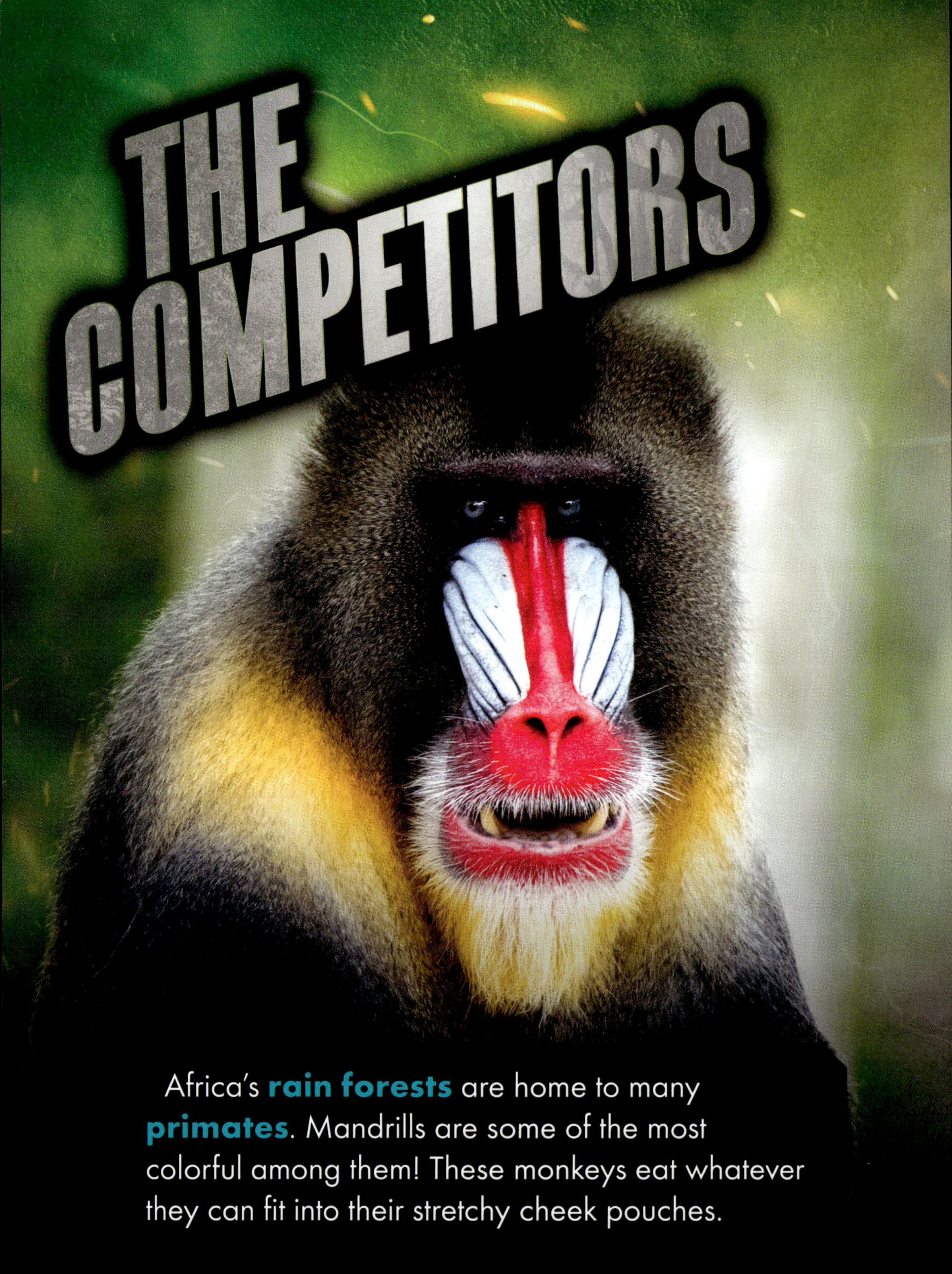

Africa's **rain forests** are home to many **primates**. Mandrills are some of the most colorful among them! These monkeys eat whatever they can fit into their stretchy cheek pouches.

Mandrills share these rain forests with chimpanzees. These **apes** use teamwork and tools to outsmart **prey** and enemies. Which primate rules the rain forest?

Mandrills are the world's largest monkeys. They grow up to 3 feet (1 meter) long. They weigh up to 77 pounds (35 kilograms). The monkeys have golden beards and small eyes. Their noses and mouths are blue and red.

Mandrills are found in the rain forests of west-central Africa. They can live in groups of up to 200 members.

LOUD AND ROWDY

Mandrill groups are noisy. They often talk to each other using grunts and high-pitched screams!

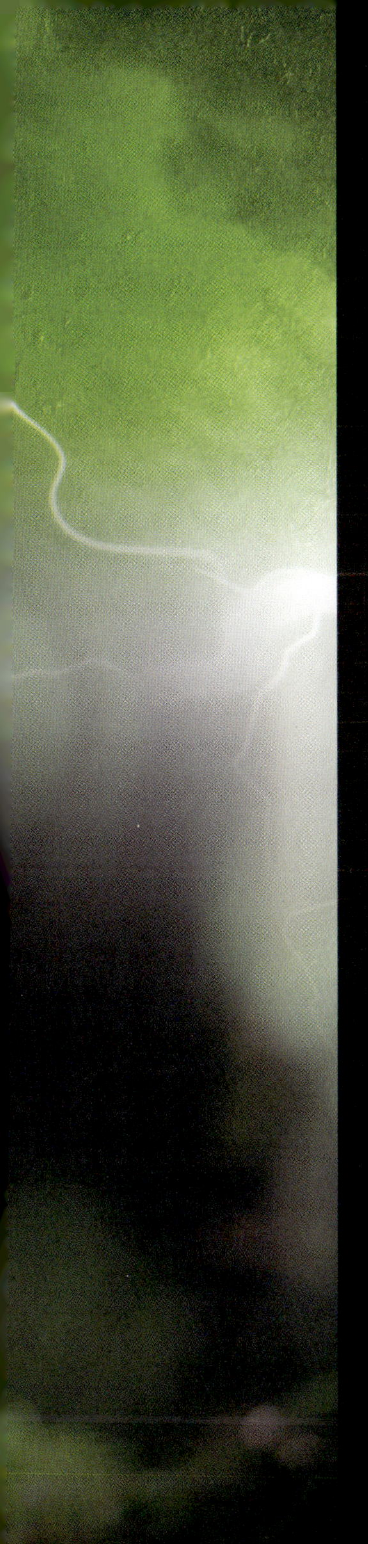

MANDRILL PROFILE

LENGTH

UP TO 3 FEET
(1 METER)

WEIGHT

UP TO 77 POUNDS
(35 KILOGRAMS)

HABITATS

FORESTS

RAIN FORESTS

MANDRILL RANGE

CHIMPANZEE PROFILE

HEIGHT
UP TO 5.5 FEET
(1.7 METERS)
ON BACK LEGS

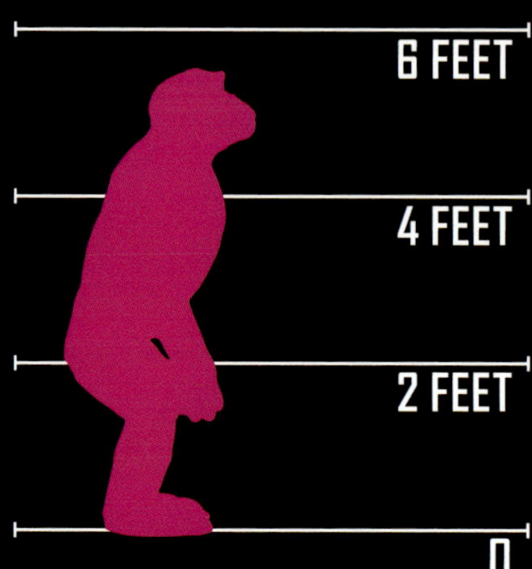

WEIGHT
UP TO 130 POUNDS
(59 KILOGRAMS)

HABITATS

FORESTS

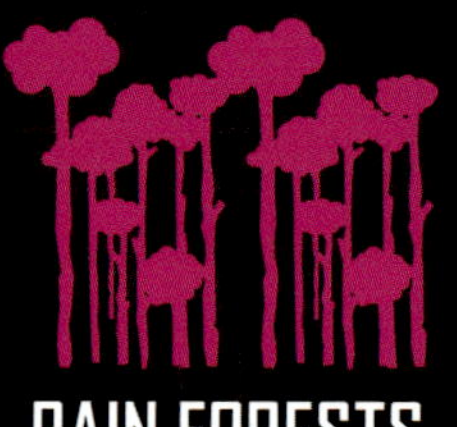
RAIN FORESTS

SAVANNAS

CHIMPANZEE RANGE

Chimpanzees are some of the smartest apes. They live throughout west and central Africa's **savannas** and forests. They are highly social. The apes live in groups that can have as few as 20 and as many as 100 members.

Chimpanzees can stand up to 5.5 feet (1.7 meters) tall on their back legs, but they often walk on all fours. Their arms are longer than their legs. Brownish-black hair covers most of their bodies.

OUR CLOSEST RELATIVE

Chimpanzees are humans' closest animal relatives.

SECRET WEAPONS

Mandrills have long, powerful arms. They use these to **forage** for food on the ground and in trees. Their arms also help them climb trees quickly to escape danger.

Chimpanzees are smart animals. Their **intelligence** helps them solve problems and outsmart **predators**. It also allows the apes to use tools. They use rocks and branches to find food.

BRAIN SIZE COMPARISON

CHIMPANZEE
0.85 POUNDS
(0.39 KILOGRAMS)

HUMAN
3 POUNDS
(1.4 KILOGRAMS)

Mandrills have large, sharp **canine teeth**. These grow up to 2.5 inches (6.4 centimeters) long. The monkeys use them to give painful bites to enemies.

Chimpanzees use teamwork. Groups of male chimpanzees patrol home areas looking for prey and enemies. They use a hunting bark to call more members to help them hunt. This teamwork helps keep the apes full and safe!

SECRET WEAPONS

MANDRILL

Mandrills have **opposable thumbs**. They use these to help them climb trees and grab food. The monkeys are able to turn over rocks and pick up fruits and seeds.

Chimpanzees use their opposable thumbs to grab branches. This helps them climb trees. The apes can also easily grab food and hold tools.

ATTACK MOVES

Mandrills try to scare enemies. They stare them down. The monkeys slap the ground and charge. They also jump up and down.

Chimpanzees use tools to deadly effect. They use sticks to collect **insects** from mounds. They sharpen sticks into spears to hunt small **mammals**. The apes also crack nuts open with rocks.

TORTOISE SMASHERS

Chimpanzees have been seen slamming tortoises into trees to open their shells.

Mandrills show their teeth to scare off enemies. They open their mouths wide as if they are yawning. If enemies get too close, mandrills will bite.

MOODY MONKEYS

The colors on a mandrill's nose and mouth become brighter when the monkeys are excited or angry.

Chimpanzees chase smaller prey. Groups often spread out to find and trap prey. The apes also attack other chimpanzee groups that come too close.

READY, FIGHT!

A mandrill stuffs its cheeks with fruit. But a nearby chimpanzee wants the fruit, too! The monkey slaps the ground to scare the chimpanzee. But the chimpanzee calls for its group.

The mandrill bites a chimpanzee. But the group surrounds it. They hit and stomp the mandrill until they can grab the fruit. The chimpanzees used teamwork to steal a meal!

GLOSSARY

apes—large primates that lack a tail

canine teeth—long, pointed teeth that are often the sharpest in the mouth

forage—to search for food

insects—small animals with six legs and hard outer bodies; an insect's body is divided into three parts.

intelligence—the ability to learn or understand

mammals—warm-blooded animals that have backbones and feed their young milk

opposable thumbs—thumbs that allow animals to hold and handle objects; opposable thumbs are commonly found on primates.

predators—animals that hunt other animals for food

prey—animals that are hunted by other animals for food

primates—any of a group of mammals that includes humans, apes, and monkeys

rain forests—thick, green forests that receive a lot of rain

savannas—flat grasslands in Africa with very few trees

TO LEARN MORE

AT THE LIBRARY

Markovics, Joyce. *Apes.* Ann Arbor, Mich.: Cherry Lake Publishing, 2023.

Rose, Rachel. *Mandrill.* Minneapolis, Minn.: Bearport Publishing, 2022.

Sommer, Nathan. *Komodo Dragon vs. Orangutan.* Minneapolis, Minn.: Bellwether Media, 2021.

ON THE WEB

FACTSURFER

Factsurfer.com gives you a safe, fun way to find more information.

1. Go to www.factsurfer.com
2. Enter "mandrill vs. chimpanzee" into the search box and click 🔍.
3. Select your book cover to see a list of related content.

INDEX

The images in this book are reproduced through the courtesy of: Natalia Paklina, front cover (mandrill); Edwin Butter, front cover (chimpanzee); Manon van Althuis, p. 4; KensCanning, p. 5; mbrand85, pp. 6-7; Abeselom Zerit, pp. 8-9; GE2J72/ Alamy, p. 10; Danny Ye, p. 11; Andy Crocker, p. 12; Juergen Ritterbach/ Alamy, p. 13; Avalon.red/ Alamy, p. 14; Lapis2380, p. 14 (powerful arms); dwphotos, p. 14 (sharp canine teeth); michael meijer, p. 14 (opposable thumbs); Joshua Davenport, p. 15; anek.soowannaphoom, p. 15 (intelligence); Alexwilko, p. 15 (teamwork); NaturesMomentsuk, p. 15 (opposable thumbs); by toonman/ Getty, p. 16; Fuse/Getty, p. 17; Tanya Puntti, p. 18; Foto Mous, p. 19; Hit1912, pp. 20-21; Steffen Foerster, pp. 20-21.